# THE WORLD'S SEXIEST CUPCAKES BROUGHT TO YOU BY THE WORLD'S MOST DELICIOUS BAKERS

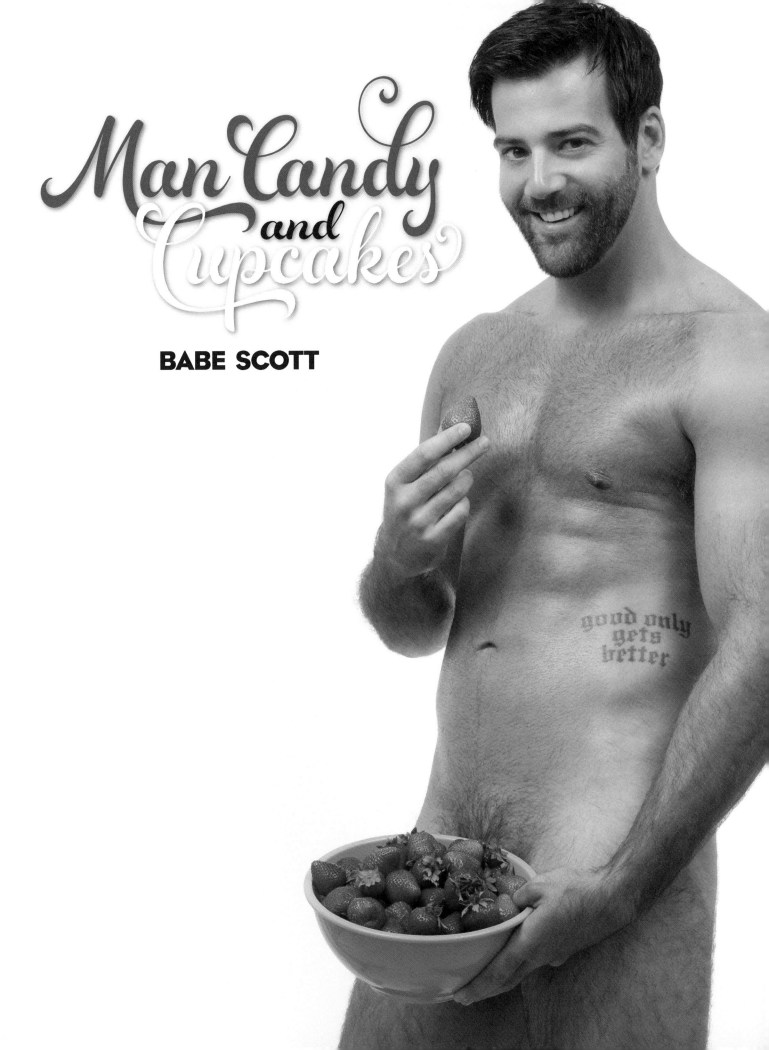

# Man Candy and Cupcakes

**BABE SCOTT**

**Published by Babe Media, LLC**

Printed in the United States

**ISBN** 978-0-9844527-5-0


**Photography** Babe Scott

**Design** Sharon Metzl

**First Edition**

For more information, visit **Babe**'s website at babescott.com

# Man Candy and Cupcakes

# BRINGING BRAWN TOBAKING

This book combines my all-time favorite things—cupcakes and cute guys (the first goes straight to my thighs, while I only wish the other would). I've long had a passion for cupcakes but felt that no recipe book had ever explored their sensual side.

These seemingly innocent sweet treats have seductive powers you never even knew existed. Sure, by day, they show their cutesy side at kids' parties and girly get-togethers, but once the sun goes down, they are just plain naughty.

If you want to seduce someone, nothing takes less effort or has more effect than these after-dark cupcakes. From the first moist and creamy mouthful, he or she will be putty in your arms. Trust me, more than the batter will be rising!

These risqué recipes are so irresistible they should only be shared between consenting adults. If you want to enjoy these tempting treats alone, make sure you add batteries to your list of baking supplies.

And that's just the cupcakes! I've also scoured the country to find the sexiest bakers of all time. Just call it a labor of lust! My buffed bakers will ignite not only your taste buds, but all of your senses.

These hot hunks will bring your culinary fantasies to life! Each baker sizzles in his own unique way and isn't afraid to leave his personality (or his shirtless torso) on the page.

First up is the **Cowboy Cupcake**, who will take your taste buds on a wild ride. He's followed by the **Bad Boy Baker**, a modern-day Marlon Brando armed with a mixer. Next is the **Baker Next Door**, who will melt your heart with his sentimental cupcakes. And finally, the **Castaway Cupcake** will make you want to taste forbidden flavors.

*Man Candy and Cupcakes* is guaranteed to get you drooling!

Bakers make it rise!

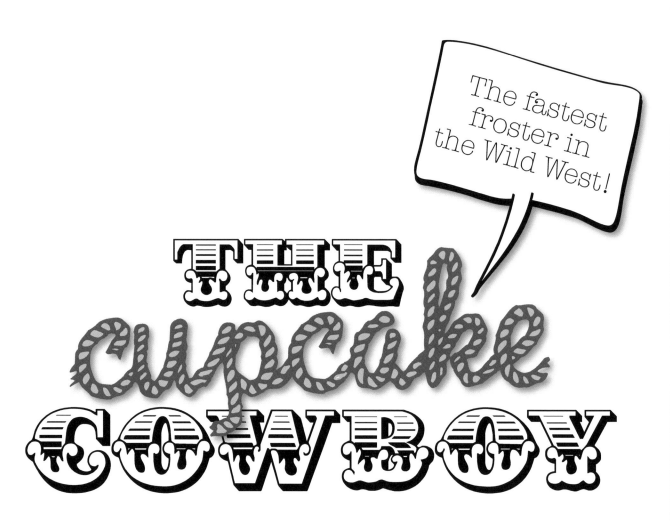

The fastest froster in the Wild West!

# THE cupcake COWBOY

This bronco-busting baker is
at home behind the range.
His homespun cupcakes
will have you chomping
at the bit for more.

# Lonesome Cowboy Cupcake

The combination of salty and sweet makes this salted caramel cupcake (and this cowboy) an irresistible combination.

## Salted Caramel Cupcakes with Caramel Buttercream

MAKES 12

### SALTED CARAMEL CUPCAKES

**Ingredients**

- 2 cups all-purpose flour
- 1½ teaspoons baking powder
- ½ teaspoon salt
- ½ cup (1 stick) unsalted butter, room temperature
- 1½ cups sugar
- 2 eggs, room temperature
- 2 teaspoons vanilla extract
- ¾ cup milk

1. Preheat oven to 350 degrees F and line 12 muffin cups with paper liners.

2. In a medium bowl, whisk together flour, baking powder and salt and set aside.

3. In a large bowl, beat butter and sugar with a mixer until light and fluffy. Add the eggs, one at a time, beating well after each addition. Add vanilla and mix again.

4. Reduce mixer speed to low. Add the dry ingredients to the butter mixture in two parts, alternating with milk, and mix until all is combined.

5. Evenly fill muffin cups with batter and bake for 18-20 minutes or until a toothpick inserted into the center comes out clean. Let cool for about 10 minutes before frosting.

### CARAMEL SAUCE

**Ingredients**

- ½ cup (1 stick) unsalted butter
- 1½ cups packed dark brown sugar
- ¾ cup light brown sugar
- ¾ cup whole milk

1. In a large saucepan over medium heat, stir together butter, sugars and milk and bring to a boil. Continue boiling for 3 minutes.

2. Remove sauce from heat and allow to cool.

3. After cupcakes have cooled for 10 minutes, pierce with a fork about 10 times. Pour 1 tablespoon of caramel sauce on top of each cupcake, allowing it to drip into the holes.

4. Reserve the rest of the sauce to make buttercream and popcorn toppers.

### CARAMEL BUTTERCREAM

**Ingredients**

- ¾ cup reserved caramel sauce, cooled
- 4 tablespoons unsalted butter, room temperature
- 2½–3 cups confectioners' sugar
- 2 tablespoons milk

1. In a medium bowl, beat caramel sauce and butter with a mixer until combined. Add sugar, one cup at a time, beating after each addition. Add milk and beat until smooth.

### CARAMEL POPCORN

**Ingredients**

- 2 cups popped popcorn
- ⅓ cup reserved caramel sauce

1. Line a baking sheet with aluminum foil.

2. Toss popped popcorn with caramel sauce until covered. Spread evenly across baking sheet and allow to dry for 10-20 minutes.

3. Let the cupcakes cool completely. Pipe caramel buttercream on top using a pastry bag and tip or a plastic bag with the corner snipped off.

4. Garnish with a few pieces of caramel popcorn and sprinkle with sea salt.

### ASSEMBLY

Let the cupcakes cool completely. Pipe caramel buttercream on top using a pastry bag and tip or a plastic bag with the corner snipped off. Garnish with a few pieces of caramel popcorn and sprinkle with sea salt.

# I'm Nuts For You

If you like peanut butter as much as you like perfect pecs, then you will go nuts for this delicious peanut butter cupcake.

## Reese's Peanut Butter Cupcakes with Peanut Butter Frosting

MAKES 12

### PEANUT BUTTER CUPCAKES

**Ingredients**

2 cups all-purpose flour

½ teaspoon baking powder

½ teaspoon baking soda

½ teaspoon salt

¼ teaspoon ground cinnamon

⅓ cup unsalted butter, room temperature

½ cup peanut butter

1¼ cups packed brown sugar

1 egg, room temperature

1 teaspoon vanilla extract

¾ cup milk

12 miniature Reese's peanut butter cups, unwrapped

1. Preheat oven to 350 degrees F and line 12 muffin cups with paper liners.

2. In a medium bowl, whisk together flour, baking powder, baking soda, salt and cinnamon and set aside.

3. In a large bowl, beat butter, peanut butter and brown sugar with a mixer until light and fluffy. Beat in egg and vanilla.

4. Reduce mixer speed to low. Add the dry ingredients to the butter mixture in two parts, alternating with milk, and mix until all is combined.

5. Fill muffin cups about two-thirds full with batter. Press a peanut butter cup into the center of each until the top is even with the batter. Bake for 20-22 minutes or until a toothpick inserted into the cupcake come out clean. Let cool completely before frosting.

### PEANUT BUTTER FROSTING

**Ingredients**

⅓ cup unsalted butter, room temperature

⅓ cup creamy peanut butter

1½ teaspoons vanilla extract

2 cups confectioners' sugar

¼ teaspoon salt

3 tablespoons milk

1. In a medium bowl, beat butter and peanut butter with a mixer until creamy. Add vanilla and mix until combined. Add sugar, one cup at a time. Add salt and milk and mix until light and fluffy.

2. Pipe on top of cooled cupcakes using a pastry bag and tip or plastic bag with the corner snipped off.

**To make your own chocolate horse, visit the Cupcake Decorations section of my blog at *ManCandyandCupcakes. com* for directions.**

## Chocolate Bourbon Cupcakes with Whiskey Chocolate Buttercream

MAKES 12

### CHOCOLATE BOURBON CUPCAKES

**Ingredients**

½ cup unsweetened cocoa powder

½ cup boiling water

1½ cups all-purpose flour

1 teaspoon baking powder

½ teaspoon baking soda

½ teaspoon salt

½ cup (1 stick) butter, room temperature

1½ cups sugar

2 eggs, room temperature

1 teaspoon vanilla extract

¾ cup buttermilk

½ cup bourbon

1. Preheat oven to 350 degrees F and line 12 muffin cups with paper liners.

2. In a small bowl, mix cocoa with boiling water until dissolved. Set aside to cool.

3. In a medium bowl, whisk together flour, baking powder, baking soda and salt and set aside.

4. In a large bowl, beat butter and sugar with a mixer until light and fluffy. Add the eggs, one at a time, beating well after each addition. Add vanilla and mix again.

5. Reduce mixer speed to low. Add the dry ingredients to the butter mixture in three parts, alternating with the buttermilk and bourbon, and mix until all is combined.

6. Add the cooled cocoa mixture and mix until smooth.

7. Evenly fill muffin cups with batter and bake for 18-20 minutes or until a toothpick inserted into the center comes out clean. Let cool completely before frosting.

### WHISKEY CHOCOLATE BUTTERCREAM

**Ingredients**

½ cup (1 stick) unsalted butter, room temperature

⅓ cup unsweetened cocoa powder

2 tablespoons whiskey

2 cups confectioners' sugar

1. In a medium bowl, beat butter and cocoa with a mixer until light and fluffy. Add the whiskey and beat again. Add sugar, one cup at a time, beating after each addition.

2. Pipe on top of cooled cupcakes using a pastry bag and tip or plastic bag with the corner snipped off.

**To make your own fondant sheriff's badge, visit the Cupcake Decorations section of my blog at *ManCandyandCupcakes.com* for directions.**

# Surrender Now Cupcake

Step away, step away from the cupcake...This delicious chocolate bourbon cupcake is so delicious, it's darned criminal. Let's hope this sheriff frisks you to find out where you keep yours stashed.

## Hazelnut Cupcakes with Espresso Frangelico Buttercream

MAKES 12

### HAZELNUT CUPCAKES

**Ingredients**

1½ cups all-purpose flour

1 teaspoon baking powder

½ teaspoon baking soda

½ teaspoon salt

½ cup ground hazelnuts (instructions follow)

½ cup (1 stick) unsalted butter, room temperature

1 cup sugar

2 eggs, room temperature

½ cup brewed hazelnut coffee

1 tablespoon Frangelico

1. Preheat oven to 350 degrees F and line 12 muffin cups with paper liners.

2. In a medium bowl, whisk together flour, baking powder, baking soda and salt. Stir in ground hazelnuts and set aside.

3. In large bowl, beat butter and sugar with a mixer until light and fluffy. Add the eggs, one at a time, beating well after each addition.

4. Reduce mixer speed to low. Add the dry ingredients to the butter mixture in two parts, alternating with the hazelnut coffee, and mix until all is combined. Add Frangelico and beat until smooth.

5. Evenly fill muffin cups with batter and bake for 15-18 minutes or until a toothpick inserted into the center comes out clean. Let cool completely before frosting.

### TOASTED HAZELNUTS

**Ingredients**

1 cup hazelnuts

1. Preheat oven to 350 degrees F. Place hazelnuts on a baking sheet and toast for 5-6 minutes, until skins turn dark and start to crack.

2. Allow to cool slightly and then wrap in a clean kitchen towel. Rub between your hands for 10-20 seconds until the skins fall off. Pulse hazelnuts in a food processor until ground.

## Rope Those Calves

Our baker likes roping your calves as much as he does making cupcakes. This hazelnut cupcake will lasso your taste buds.

### ESPRESSO FRANGELICO BUTTERCREAM

**Ingredients**

½ cup (1 stick) unsalted butter, room temperature

3 cups confectioners' sugar

2 tablespoons espresso powder

1 tablespoon Frangelico

1. In a medium bowl, beat the butter with a mixer until smooth. Add sugar, one cup at a time, beating after each addition. Add espresso powder and Frangelico and beat until smooth.

2. Pipe on top of cooled cupcakes using a pastry bag and tip or plastic bag with the corner snipped off.

**To make your own fondant cow skull, visit the Cupcake Decorations section of my blog at *ManCandyandCupcakes.com* for directions.**

# You Make My Knees Buckle

This classic spiced pumpkin cupcake will make you go weak at the knees. After a serving of this you will want to ride into the sunset with our baker, saddle or not.

## Spiced Pumpkin Cupcakes with Cream Cheese Frosting

MAKES 12

### SPICED PUMPKIN CUPCAKES

**Ingredients**

1½ cups all-purpose flour

1 teaspoon baking powder

½ teaspoon baking soda

½ teaspoon salt

1 teaspoon ground cinnamon

1 teaspoon ground ginger

¼ teaspoon ground nutmeg

¼ teaspoon allspice

½ cup (1 stick) unsalted butter, room temperature

1 cup sugar

2 eggs, room temperature

1 teaspoon vanilla extract

½ cup canned pumpkin

¼ cup sweetened condensed milk

1. Preheat oven to 350 degrees F and line 12 muffin cups with paper liners.

2. In a medium bowl, whisk together flour, baking powder, baking soda, salt, cinnamon, ginger, nutmeg and allspice and set aside.

3. In a large bowl, beat butter and sugar with a mixer until light and fluffy. Add the eggs, one at a time, beating well after each addition. Add vanilla and mix again.

4. Reduce mixer speed to low. Add the dry ingredients to the butter mixture in three parts, alternating with canned pumpkin and condensed milk, and mix until all is combined. Do not overbeat.

5. Evenly fill muffin cups with batter and bake for 18-20 minutes or until a toothpick inserted into the center comes out clean. Let cool completely before frosting.

### CREAM CHEESE FROSTING

**Ingredients**

8 ounces cream cheese, softened

½ cup (1 stick) unsalted butter, room temperature

3 cups confectioners' sugar

½ teaspoon vanilla extract

1. In a medium bowl, beat cream cheese and butter with a mixer until light and fluffy. Add sugar, one cup at a time, beating after each addition. Add vanilla and mix until smooth.

2. Pipe on top of cooled cupcakes using a pastry bag and tip or plastic bag with the corner snipped off.

**To make your own fondant cowboy hat, visit the Cupcake Decorations section of my blog at *ManCandyandCupcakes.com* for directions.**

## Apple Cider Cupcakes with Apple Cider Cream Cheese Frosting

MAKES 24

### APPLE CIDER CUPCAKES

**Ingredients**

2½ cups all-purpose flour

1 teaspoon baking powder

½ teaspoon baking soda

½ teaspoon salt

1 teaspoon cinnamon

½ cup (1 stick) unsalted butter, room temperature

1½ cups sugar

2 eggs, room temperature

1 teaspoon vanilla extract

½ cup apple cider

2 cups peeled and chopped apples (about two medium apples)

1. Preheat oven to 350 degrees F and line 24 muffin cups with paper liners.

2. In a medium bowl, whisk together flour, baking powder, baking soda, salt and cinnamon and set aside.

3. In a large bowl, beat butter and sugar until light and fluffy. Add the eggs, one at a time, beating well after each addition. Add vanilla and mix again.

4. Reduce mixer speed to low. Add the flour mixture to the butter mixture in three parts, alternating with the apple cider, and mix until all is combined. Fold in chopped apples.

5. Evenly fill muffin cups with batter and bake for 20-22 minutes or until a toothpick inserted into the center comes out clean. Let cool completely before frosting.

# Real Cupcakes Wear Plaid

This homespun sweet is the cupcake version of the plaid shirt. It's classic country and packs a punch when it comes to flavor.

### APPLE CIDER CREAM CHEESE FROSTING

**Ingredients**

8 ounces cream cheese, softened

¼ cup (½ stick) unsalted butter, room temperature

2½ cups confectioners' sugar

¼ cup apple cider

1. In a medium bowl, beat cream cheese and butter with a mixer until light and fluffy. Add sugar, one cup at a time, beating after each addition. Add apple cider and beat until smooth.

2. Pipe on top of cooled cupcakes using a pastry bag and tip or plastic bag with the corner snipped off.

**To make your own edible plaid topper, visit the Cupcake Decorations section of my blog at *ManCandyandCupcakes. com* for directions.**

# Blue For You Cupcake

The best cure for the boyfriend blues is a blue velvet cupcake. This decadent dessert will make you forget any fight and find that loving feeling again.

## Blue Velvet Cupcakes with Jack Daniel's Cream Cheese Frosting
MAKES 12

### BLUE VELVET CUPCAKES

**Ingredients**

- 2½ cups all-purpose flour
- 2 tablespoons cocoa powder
- ½ teaspoon salt
- 1½ cups sugar
- 1½ cups vegetable oil
- 2 eggs, room temperature
- 1 teaspoon vanilla extract
- 2 teaspoons blue gel food paste
- 1 cup buttermilk
- 2 teaspoons white vinegar
- 1½ teaspoons baking soda

1. Preheat oven to 350 degrees F and line 12 muffin cups with paper liners.

2. In a large bowl, sift together flour, cocoa powder and salt and set aside.

3. In another bowl, beat sugar and vegetable oil together with a mixer. Add eggs, one at a time, mixing well after each addition. Add vanilla and blue gel paste and mix well.

4. Add the dry ingredients to the sugar mixture, alternating with the buttermilk. Mix well after each addition.

5. In a small bowl add the vinegar to the baking soda and stir well. (There should be a slight bubbling reaction.) Add this into the batter and mix well.

6. Fill muffin cups two-thirds full with batter and bake for 20 minutes or until a toothpick inserted into the center comes out clean. Let cool completely before frosting.

### JACK DANIEL'S CREAM CHEESE FROSTING

**Ingredients**

- ½ cup (1 stick) unsalted butter, softened
- 8 ounces cream cheese, softened
- 3 cups confectioners' sugar
- 3 tablespoons Jack Daniel's

1. In a mixing bowl beat butter and cream cheese together with a mixer until light and fluffy. Add the confectioners' sugar, one cup at a time, beating after each addition. Add the Jack Daniel's and mix until smooth.

2. Pipe frosting on top of cooled cupcakes with a piping bag and tip or plastic bag with the tip snipped off.

**To make your own fondant cowboy boot, visit the Cupcake Decorations section of my blog at *ManCandyandCupcakes.com* for directions.**

## Jalapeño Peach Cupcakes with Peach Cream Cheese Frosting

MAKES 12

### JALAPEÑO PEACH CUPCAKES

**Ingredients**

- 2 cups all-purpose flour
- ½ teaspoon salt
- 1½ teaspoons baking powder
- ½ cup (1 stick) unsalted butter, room temperature
- 1½ cups sugar
- 2 eggs, room temperature
- 1 teaspoon vanilla extract
- ¾ cup peach nectar or juice
- 2 jalapeños, finely chopped
- ½ cup peach jam or preserves, for filling

1. Preheat the oven to 350 degrees F and line 12 muffin cups with paper liners.

2. In a medium bowl, whisk together flour, salt, and baking powder and set aside.

3. In a large bowl, beat butter and sugar with a mixer until light and fluffy. Add the eggs, one a time, beating well after each addition. Add vanilla and jalapeños and stir to combine.

4. Reduce mixer speed to low. Add the dry ingredients to the butter mixture in three parts, alternating with peach nectar, and mix until all is combined.

5. Evenly fill muffin cups with batter and bake for 18-20 minutes or until a toothpick inserted into the center comes out clean. Let cool completely before filling.

6. Using an apple corer, remove the center of each cupcake, being careful not to pierce the bottom. Spoon 1 teaspoon of peach preserves into each cupcake.

### PEACH CREAM CHEESE FROSTING

**Ingredients**

- 8 ounces cream cheese, softened
- ¼ cup (½ stick) unsalted butter, room temperature
- 1½ teaspoons vanilla extract
- 4 cups confectioners' sugar
- ¼ cup peach jam or preserves

1. In a medium bowl, beat cream cheese and butter with a mixer until fluffy. Add vanilla and mix until combined. Add sugar, one cup at a time, beating after each addition. Add peach jam and mix again.

2. Pipe on top of cooled cupcakes using a pastry bag and tip or plastic bag with the corner snipped off.

**To recreate my desert-inspired decorations and for directions on baking in terracotta pots, visit the Cupcake Decorations section of my blog at *ManCandyandCupcakes. com* for directions.**

# Cactus Blooms Cupcake

If you want to show your sweetheart that your love blooms like a desert cactus, then this is the cupcake for you. A hit of spicy jalapeño brings out the wild side of this fragrant peach treat.

## Bread Pudding Cupcakes with Cinnamon Cream Cheese Frosting

MAKES 12

### BREAD PUDDING CUPCAKES

**Ingredients**

5 eggs, room temperature

¾ cup milk

¾ cup sugar

1½ teaspoons vanilla extract

1 teaspoon cinnamon

2½ cups brioche cut into ½-inch cubes

½ cup whiskey-soaked raisins (recipe follows)

1. Preheat oven to 350 degrees F and line 12 muffin cups with paper liners.

2. In a large bowl, whisk together eggs, milk, sugar, vanilla and cinnamon. Add brioche cubes and allow to sit for 5-10 minutes to absorb the mixture. Stir in whiskey-soaked raisins.

3. Fill muffin cups completely full with bread pudding. Bake for 22-25 minutes. Let cool completely before frosting.

# Lucky in Love

This bread pudding cupcake just melts in your mouth. It's rustic charm will have you swooning.

### WHISKEY-SOAKED RAISINS

**Ingredients**

½ cup raisins

5 tablespoons whiskey

1. Place raisins in a bowl and pour whiskey over the top to cover. Let stand for at least an hour before using.

### CINNAMON CREAM CHEESE FROSTING

**Ingredients**

8 ounces cream cheese, softened

5 tablespoons unsalted butter, room temperature

1½ teaspoons vanilla extract

3 cups confectioners' sugar

2 teaspoons cinnamon

1. In medium bowl, beat cream cheese and butter with a mixer until light and fluffy. Add sugar, one cup at a time, beating after each addition. Add vanilla and cinnamon and mix until smooth.

2. Pipe on top of cooled cupcakes using a pastry bag and tip or plastic bag with the corner snipped off.

**To make your own fondant horseshoe, visit the Cupcake Decorations section of my blog at *ManCandyandCupcakes. com* for directions.**

# Cowboy Dreams Cupcake

This maple cheeesecake cupcake will make you dream of a land before cell phones and schedules, where coyotes howl and cowboys rule.

## Maple Cheesecake Cupcakes with Strawberry Sauce
MAKES 12

### MAPLE CHEESECAKE CUPCAKES

**Ingredients**

**For Crust**
- 1 cup graham crackers
- 3 tablespoons sugar
- 3 tablespoons unsalted butter, melted
- ¾ cup strawberry preserves

**For Filling**
- 16 ounces cream cheese, softened
- ¾ cup maple syrup
- 2 tablespoons sugar
- 2 eggs
- 2 teaspoons vanilla extract
- 4 tablespoons flour

1. Preheat oven to 275 degrees F and line 12 muffin cups with paper liners.

**Make crust**

1. To make the graham cracker crumbs, crush graham crackers in a food processor or in a plastic bag with a rolling pin, until finely ground. In a medium bowl, mix together graham cracker crumbs, sugar and melted butter until well combined. Put a heaping tablespoon into the bottom of each paper liner and press down with the back of a teaspoon. Add one tablespoon of strawberry preserves on top of each crust.

**Make filling**

1. In a medium bowl, beat the cream cheese with a mixer until light and fluffy. Reduce mixer speed to low and drizzle in the maple syrup until combined. Beat in sugar, egg, vanilla and flour until smooth.

2. Pour the mixture over the crumb crusts almost to the top. Bake for 30-35 minutes or until set. Let cool completely before frosting.

### STRAWBERRY SAUCE

**Ingredients**
- 1 pint strawberries, hulled (plus extra for garnish)
- ¼ cup sugar
- 1 teaspoon balsamic vinegar
- 4 tablespoons water
- 1 teaspoon cornstarch

1. Combine strawberries, sugar, balsamic vinegar and 2 tablespoons of water in a saucepan and bring to a simmer over medium heat.

2. Reduce heat to medium-low and simmer for 15 minutes.

3. In a separate bowl whisk together the remaining 2 tablespoons of water and cornstarch.

4. Whisk cornstarch mixture into strawberry mixture. Cook, stirring constantly, until mixture thickens about 2 to 3 minutes. Remove from heat.

5. Allow mixture to cool slightly. Transfer to a blender and purée until smooth.

6. Drizzle sauce on top of cooled cupcakes. Garnish with a strawberry.

# Banana Walnut Cupcakes with Chocolate Molasses Frosting

MAKES 24

## BANANA WALNUT CUPCAKES

### Ingredients

2 cups all-purpose flour
1 teaspoon baking powder
1 teaspoon baking soda
½ teaspoon salt
½ cup (1 stick) unsalted butter, room temperature
1½ cups sugar
2 eggs, room temperature
1 teaspoon vanilla extract
3 ripe bananas, mashed with
1 teaspoon lemon juice
1 cup buttermilk
¾ cup walnuts, chopped

1. Preheat oven to 350 degrees F and line 24 muffin cups with paper liners.

2. In a medium bowl, whisk together flour, baking powder, baking soda and salt and set aside.

3. In a large bowl, beat butter and sugar with a mixer until light and fluffy. Add the eggs, one a time, beating well after each addition. Add vanilla and beat again. Add mashed banana and mix until combined.

4. Reduce mixer speed to low. Add the dry ingredients to the butter mixture in two parts, alternating with the buttermilk, and mix until all is combined. Fold in chopped walnuts.

5. Evenly fill muffin cups with batter and bake for 18-20 minutes or until a toothpick inserted into the center comes out clean. Let cool completely before frosting.

## CHOCOLATE MOLASSES FROSTING

### Ingredients

8 ounces cream cheese
¼ cup (½ stick) unsalted butter, room temperature
¼ cup unsweetened cocoa powder
3 cups confectioners' sugar
¼ cup molasses
1 teaspoon vanilla extract

1. In a large bowl, beat cream cheese and butter with a mixer until light and fluffy. Add cocoa and mix to combine. Add sugar, one cup at a time, beating after each addition. Add molasses and vanilla and beat until smooth.

2. Pipe on top of cooled cupcakes using a pastry bag and tip or plastic bag with the corner snipped off. Top with a banana slice.

## Happy Trails Cupcake

Banana and walnuts go together like the Lone Ranger and Tonto. This cowboylicious cupcake is so irresistible you will want to go back for more.

Go on. Take a bite! I know you want to

# the BadBoy BAKER

The Bad Boy Baker is the Brando of baking. This Harley-riding, hell-raising hunk will get more than the batter rising. A master of kitchen discipline, he's very handy with a spatula and not frightened to use it. His sinfully delicious recipes will take you from bike to bar room to the bedroom. Being bad never tasted so good!

# Pound Me Cupcake

This macho pound cupcake is rich, moist and silky on the tongue. Combine it with amaretto cream cheese frosting and the combination is as irresistible as Brando himself.

## Pound Cupcakes with Amaretto Buttercream

MAKES 12

### POUND CAKE CUPCAKES

**Ingredients**

3 eggs, room temperature

3 tablespoons milk

1½ teaspoons vanilla extract

1½ cups cake flour

1 teaspoon baking powder

¼ teaspoon salt

¾ cup sugar

13 tablespoons (1 stick + 1 tablespoon) unsalted butter, room temperature

1. Preheat oven to 350 degrees F and line 12 muffin cups with paper liners.

2. In a medium bowl, whisk together eggs, milk and vanilla and set aside.

3. In a large bowl, whisk flour, baking powder, salt and sugar. Add the butter and half the egg mixture and beat with a mixer on low speed until the dry ingredients are moistened.

4. Add the remaining egg mixture in two parts, beating after each addition.

5. Evenly fill muffin cups with batter and bake for 15-20 minutes or until a toothpick inserted into the center comes out clean. Let cool completely before frosting.

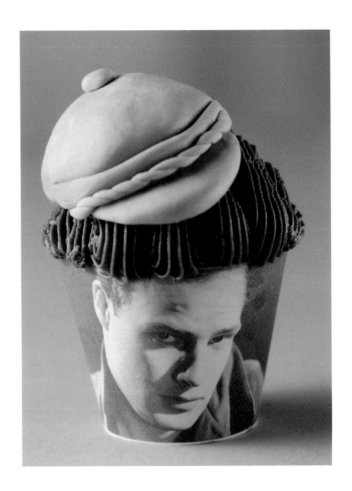

### AMARETTO BUTTERCREAM

**Ingredients**

½ cup (1 stick) unsalted butter, room temperature

3 cups confectioners' sugar

¼ cup milk

2 tablespoons amaretto

1. In a medium bowl, beat the butter with a mixer until creamy. Add sugar, one cup at a time, beating after each addition. Add milk and amaretto and beat until light and fluffy.

2. Pipe on top of cooled cupcakes using a pastry bag and tip or plastic bag with the corner snipped off.

**To make your own Brando-inspired decorations, visit the Cupcake Decorations section of my blog at *ManCandyandCupcakes. com* for directions.**

# A Salt and Battery

This delicious beer cupcake combines the world's most dependable aphrodisiac with seductive salty caramel frosting. It will pick you up in no time!

## Beer Cupcakes with Caramel Frosting

MAKES 12

### BEER CUPCAKES

**Ingredients**

1¾ cups all-purpose flour

1 teaspoon baking powder

¼ teaspoon baking soda

¼ teaspoon salt

½ cup (1 stick) unsalted butter, room temperature

1¼ cup sugar

2 eggs, room temperature

1 teaspoon vanilla extract

½ cup sour cream

½ cup stout beer, room temperature

1. Preheat oven to 350 degrees F and line 12 muffin cups with paper liners.

2. In a medium bowl, whisk together flour, baking powder, baking soda and salt and set aside.

3. In a large bowl, beat butter and sugar with a mixer until light and fluffy. Add the eggs, one at a time, beating well after each addition. Add vanilla and mix again.

4. Reduce mixer speed to low. Gradually add the dry ingredients to the butter mixture, alternating with the sour cream and beer, and mix until all is combined.

5. Evenly fill muffin cups with batter and bake for about 20 minutes or until a toothpick inserted into the center comes out clean. Let cool completely before frosting.

### CARAMEL FROSTING

**Ingredients**

2 ounces caramels

¼ cup heavy cream

½ cup (1 stick) unsalted butter, room temperature

3 cups confectioners' sugar

Pretzels, for garnish

1. Put caramels and cream in a microwave-safe bowl and microwave on high for 1 to 2 minutes, stirring at 30-second intervals, until smooth. Let cool until lukewarm, about 30 minutes.

2. In a medium bowl, beat butter with a mixer until creamy. Reduce mixer speed to low. Add sugar in three parts, alternating with caramel mixture, and mix until blended and smooth.

3. Pipe on top of cooled cupcakes using a pastry bag and tip or plastic bag with the corner snipped off. Garnish with a pretzel.

## Red Velvet Cupcakes with Cognac Cream Cheese Frosting

MAKES 12

### RED VELVET CUPCAKES

**Ingredients**

- 2½ cups all-purpose flour
- 2 tablespoon unsweetened cocoa powder
- ½ teaspoon salt
- 1½ cups sugar
- 1½ cups vegetable oil
- 2 eggs, room temperature
- 1 teaspoon vanilla extract
- 2 tablespoons red food coloring
- 1 cup buttermilk
- 2 teaspoons white vinegar
- 1½ teaspoons baking soda

1. Preheat oven to 350 degrees F and line 12 muffin cups with paper liners.

2. In a large bowl, whisk together flour, cocoa and salt and set aside.

3. In a large bowl, beat sugar and vegetable oil with a mixer until combined. Add the eggs, one at a time, beating well after each addition. Add vanilla and red food coloring and mix well.

4. Reduce mixer speed to low. Gradually add the dry ingredients to the sugar mixture, alternating with the buttermilk, and mix until all is combined.

5. In a small bowl, combine vinegar and baking soda. (There should be a slight bubbling reaction.) Add to the batter and mix well.

6. Evenly fill muffin cups with batter and bake for 20 minutes or until a toothpick inserted into the center comes out clean. Let cool completely before frosting.

### COGNAC CREAM CHEESE FROSTING

**Ingredients**

- 8 ounces cream cheese, softened
- ½ cup (1 stick) unsalted butter, room temperature
- 3 cups confectioners' sugar
- 3 tablespoons Cognac

1. In a medium bowl, beat cream cheese and butter with a mixer until light and fluffy. Add sugar, one cup at a time, beating after each addition. Add Cognac and mix until smooth.

2. Frost cooled cupcakes using a butter knife to create a smooth surface. Top with edible topper.

**To make your own edible Man Candy topper, visit the Cupcake Decorations section of my blog at *ManCandyandCupcakes. com* for directions.**

# Red Velvet Vice

Sinful, creamy and rich, this red velvet cupcake with Cognac-spiked cream cheese frosting could have been concocted by the devil himself. If it doesn't tempt you, then it's time to get your pulse checked.

## Dark and Stormy Cupcakes with Lime Cream Cheese Frosting

MAKES 12

### DARK AND STORMY CUPCAKES

**Ingredients**

2 ounces dark rum

4 ounces ginger beer

Splash of Rose's lime juice

1½ cups all-purpose flour

1 teaspoon baking powder

¼ teaspoon baking soda

½ teaspoon salt

2 teaspoons ground ginger

½ cup (1 stick) unsalted butter, room temperature

1 cup sugar

2 eggs, room temperature

¼ cup buttermilk

1. Preheat oven to 350 degrees F and line 12 muffin cups with paper liners.

2. Combine rum, ginger beer and Rose's lime juice to make a dark and stormy cocktail. Set aside.

3. In a medium bowl, whisk together flour, baking powder, baking soda, salt and ginger and set aside.

4. In a large bowl, beat the butter and sugar with a mixer until light and fluffy. Add the eggs, one at a time, beating well after each addition.

5. Reduce mixer speed to low. Gradually add the dry ingredients to the butter mixture, alternating with the dark and stormy cocktail, and mix until all is combined.

6. Evenly fill muffin cups with batter and bake for 18-20 minutes or until a toothpick inserted into the center comes out clean. Let cool completely before frosting.

# Dark and Stormy

If you like dark and stormy cocktails and dangerous liaisons, then this cupcake is for you. Spiked with rum and laced with ginger and lime, it will arouse your darkest desires.

### LIME CREAM CHEESE FROSTING

**Ingredients**

8 ounces cream cheese, softened

½ cup (1 stick) unsalted butter, room temperature

3-4 tablespoons Rose's lime juice

4-5 cups confectioners' sugar

Green food coloring

Crystallized ginger, for garnish

Lime slices, for garnish

1. In a medium bowl, beat cream cheese and butter with a mixer until light and fluffy. Add Rose's lime juice and beat until smooth. Add sugar, one cup at a time, beating after each addition. Stir in green food coloring to desired color.

2. Pipe on top of cooled cupcakes with a pastry bag and tip or plastic bag with the corner snipped off. Garnish with ginger and lime slice.

# Licorice Lust

Black licorice is a proven libido enhancer. This luscious licorice flavored cupcake with Sambuca-spiked frosting will get the sparks flying.

## Licorice Cupcakes with Vanilla Sambuca Buttercream

MAKES 12

### LICORICE CUPCAKES

**Ingredients**

1½ cups all-purpose flour

1 teaspoon baking powder

½ teaspoon salt

½ cup (1 stick) unsalted butter, room temperature

1 cup sugar

2 eggs, room temperature

¼ cup milk

¼ cup Sambuca

½ cup black licorice, chopped small

1. Preheat oven to 350 degrees F and line 12 muffin cups with paper liners.

2. In a medium bowl, whisk together flour, baking powder and salt and set aside.

3. In a large bowl, beat butter and sugar with a mixer until light and fluffy. Add the eggs, one at a time, beating well after each addition.

4. Reduce mixer speed to low. Add the dry ingredients to the butter mixture in two parts, alternating with the milk and Sambuca, and mix until all is combined. Fold in licorice pieces.

5. Evenly fill muffin cups with batter and bake for 20 minutes or until a toothpick inserted into the center comes out clean. Let cool completely before frosting.

### VANILLA SAMBUCA BUTTERCREAM

**Ingredients**

½ cup (1 stick) unsalted butter, room temperature

4 cups confectioners' sugar

1 teaspoon vanilla extract

4 tablespoons Sambuca

Licorice pieces, for garnish

1. In a medium bowl, beat butter with a mixer until creamy. Add sugar, one cup at a time, beating after each addition. Add vanilla and Sambuca and mix until light and fluffy.

2. Pipe on top of cooled cupcakes using a pastry bag and tip or plastic bag with the corner snipped off. Top with a piece of black licorice.

## Raspberry Jello Shot Cupcakes with Raspberry Vanilla Buttercream

MAKES 12

### RASPBERRY CUPCAKES

**Ingredients**

1½ cups all-purpose flour

1 teaspoon baking powder

½ teaspoon salt

½ cup (1 stick) unsalted butter, room temperature

1 cup sugar

2 eggs, room temperature

2 teaspoons raspberry extract

½ cup milk

3 tablespoons puréed fresh raspberries

1. Preheat oven to 350 degrees F and line 12 muffin cups with paper liners.

2. In a medium bowl, whisk together flour, baking powder and salt and set aside.

3. In a large bowl, beat butter and sugar with a mixer until light and fluffy. Add the eggs, one at a time, beating well after each addition. Add raspberry extract and mix to combine.

4. Reduce mixer speed to low. Add the dry ingredients to the butter mixture in two parts, alternating with the milk, and mix until all is combined. Add raspberry purée and mix again. The batter will be slightly pink in color.

5. Evenly fill muffin cups with batter and bake for 20-22 minutes or until a toothpick inserted into the center comes out clean. Let cool completely before frosting.

# You've Been Berry Bad

This risqué raspberry cupcake with a raspberry jello shot in the middle and swirls of decadent raspberry vanilla frosting will have you swooning.

### RASPBERRY VANILLA BUTTERCREAM

**Ingredients**

½ cup (1 stick) unsalted butter, room temperature

2 cups confectioners' sugar

¼ cup milk

1 teaspoon vanilla extract

¼ cup raspberry jam

5-6 fresh raspberries, crushed, plus extra for garnish

1. In a medium bowl, beat the butter with a mixer until smooth. Add sugar, one cup at a time, beating after each addition. Add milk and vanilla and mix until combined.

2. Gently fold in raspberry jam and crushed raspberries.

### AGAR-AGAR JELLO SHOTS

**Ingredients**

2 tablespoons agar-agar flakes or 2 teaspoons agar-agar powder

1 cup cran-raspberry juice from concentrate

¾ cup vodka

1. Place agar-agar and juice in a saucepan and let stand for 10 minutes.

2. Heat the saucepan over medium heat until the agar-agar dissolves. Remove from heat and allow to cool slightly.

3. In a separate saucepan, heat the vodka until slightly warm. Add to the agar-agar mixture and stir to combine. Allow mixture to cool to the point where the liquid is just starting to set.

### ASSEMBLY

1. Allow the cupcakes to cool and then, with an apple corer, remove the center of each cupcake, being careful not to pierce the bottom. Place cupcakes in the fridge for 20-30 minutes.

2. Prepare agar mixture as directed.

3. Remove the cupcakes from the fridge and pour the agar-agar mixture into the center of each cupcake. It should set quickly. You can speed up the process by putting the filled cupcakes back in the fridge for 5-10 minutes.

4. Once agar-agar is set, frost the cupcakes and top with fresh raspberries.

## Mudslide Cupcakes with Kahlua and Bailey's Buttercream Swirl

MAKES 12

### MUDSLIDE CUPCAKES

**Ingredients**

- 1¾ cups all-purpose flour
- 1½ teaspoons baking powder
- 1½ teaspoons baking soda
- 1 teaspoon salt
- 1 cups unsweetened cocoa powder
- 2 cups sugar
- 2 eggs, room temperature
- ½ cup vegetable oil
- 1 cup buttermilk
- 2 teaspoons vanilla extract
- 1 cup brewed coffee, hot

1. Preheat oven to 350 degrees F and line 12 muffin cups with paper liners.

2. In a large bowl, whisk together flour, baking powder, baking soda and salt. Stir in cocoa and sugar.

3. Add the eggs, oil, buttermilk and vanilla and beat with a mixer on a low speed until combined. Add the hot coffee and beat for about 1 minute.

4. Evenly fill muffin cups with batter and bake for 20 minutes or until a toothpick inserted into the center comes out clean. Let cool completely before frosting.

### KAHLUA BUTTERCREAM

**Ingredients**

- ½ cup (1 stick) unsalted butter, room temperature
- 3 cups confectioners' sugar
- 3 tablespoons unsweetened cocoa powder
- 3 tablespoons Kahlua
- 3 tablespoons brewed coffee, cooled

1. In a medium bowl, beat the butter with a mixer until creamy. Add sugar, one cup at a time, beating after each addition. Add cocoa, Kahlua and coffee and mix well.

### BAILEY'S BUTTERCREAM

**Ingredients**

- ½ cup (1 stick) unsalted butter, room temperature
- 3 cups confectioners' sugar
- 2 teaspoons vanilla extract
- 3 tablespoons Bailey's Irish Cream
- 4 ounces bittersweet chocolate, shaved.

1. In a medium bowl, beat the butter with a mixer until creamy. Add sugar, one cup at a time, beating after each addition. Add vanilla and Bailey's and mix well.

### TO FROST

1. Create a frosting swirl by filling a pastry bag or plastic bag with the corner snipped off half full with Kahlua frosting on one side and Bailey's frosting on the other. Pipe onto cooled cupcakes. Top with chocolate shavings.

# Death by Chocolate

This decadent chocolate cupcake is piled with layers of Kahlua chocolate frosting and Bailey's vanilla buttercream. It's an orgy of taste.

## Coffee and Donut Cupcakes

MAKES 12

### COFFEE CUPCAKES

**Ingredients**

1½ cups all-purpose flour

1 teaspoon baking powder

½ teaspoon salt

½ cup brewed coffee

⅛ cup milk

½ cup (1 stick) unsalted butter, room temperature

1 cup sugar

2 eggs, room temperature

½ teaspoon vanilla extract

1. Preheat oven to 350 degrees F and line 12 muffin cups with paper liners.

2. In a medium bowl, whisk together flour, baking powder and salt and set aside.

3. In a separate bowl, combine the coffee and milk and set aside.

4. In a large bowl, beat butter and sugar with a mixer until light and fluffy. Add the eggs, one at a time, beating well after each addition. Add vanilla and mix again.

# The Morning After Cupcake

This coffee and donut cupcake with coffee frosting is the perfect pick-me-up to enjoy after a long, hot, steamy night. You will want to go for a second helping!

5. Reduce mixer speed to low. Gradually add the dry ingredients to the butter mixture, alternating with the coffee and milk mixture, and mix until all is combined.

6. Evenly fill muffins cups with batter and bake for 20-22 minutes or until a toothpick inserted into the center come out clean. Let cool completely before frosting.

### COFFEE FROSTING

**Ingredients**

½ cup (1 stick) unsalted butter, room temperature

3 cups confectioners' sugar

3 tablespoons brewed coffee

½ teaspoon vanilla extract

1. In a medium bowl, beat the butter with a mixer until creamy. Add sugar, one cup at a time, beating after each addition. Add coffee and vanilla and mix until light and fluffy.

### COFFEE-GLAZED MINI DONUT TOPPERS

**Ingredients**

¼ cup whipping cream

1 tablespoon Bailey's Irish Cream (or any coffee-flavored liqueur)

2 teaspoons espresso powder or instant coffee

2 cups confectioners' sugar

12 mini donuts

Water, as needed

Chocolate sprinkles

1. In a medium bowl, whisk together cream, coffee liqueur and espresso powder until smooth. Stir in the sugar until combined. If the glaze is too thick, stir in water, ¼ teaspoon at a time.

2. Dip the top of each mini donut into the mixture and top with chocolate sprinkles. Place on a lined baking sheet and allow the glaze to set.

### ASSEMBLY

Once cupcakes have cooled, spread a layer of the coffee frosting on top and add a glazed donut.

# The Devil Made Me Chew It!

This devilish cupcake is as tempting as the horned one himself.
It's filled and frosted with a gloriously wicked midnight ganache.

## Devil's Food Cupcakes with Chocolate Ganache

MAKES 24

### DEVIL'S FOOD CUPCAKES

**Ingredients**

1¾ cups all-purpose flour

1½ teaspoons baking powder

1½ teaspoons baking soda

1 teaspoon salt

1 cup unsweetened cocoa powder

2 cups sugar

2 eggs, room temperature

½ cup vegetable oil

1 cup buttermilk

2 teaspoons vanilla extract

1 cup brewed coffee, hot

1. Preheat oven to 350 degrees F and line 24 muffin cups with paper liners.

2. In a large bowl, whisk together flour, baking powder, baking soda and salt. Add cocoa and sugar and stir to combine.

3. Add the eggs, oil, buttermilk and vanilla and beat with a mixer on a low speed until combined. Add the coffee and beat for 1 minute.

4. Evenly fill muffin cups with batter and bake for 20 minutes or until a toothpick inserted into the center comes out clean. Let cool completely before filling and frosting.

### MIDNIGHT GANACHE

**Ingredients**

1 pound (16 ounces) semisweet chocolate

½ cup heavy cream

1. Melt chocolate in a double boiler or in the microwave, one minute at a time, until smooth.

2. Warm the heavy cream in a small saucepan. Do not let it boil.

3. Add warmed cream to the melted chocolate and whisk until combined. Place in the fridge until firm.

### FILL AND FROST

1. When the cupcakes are cool, use an apple corer to gently remove the center of each one, being careful not to pierce the bottom.

2. Place the ganache in a pastry bag or in a plastic bag with the corner snipped off. Pipe the ganache into the center of each cupcake. Use the remaining ganache to frost each cupcake.

3. Garnish if you like with a white chocolate skull. I used a silicon candy mold and white fondant to create the skull.

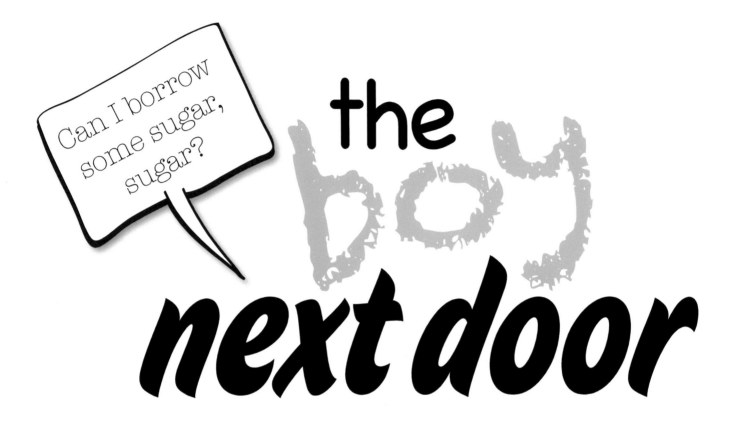

Can I borrow some sugar, sugar?

# the boy
# next door

The Baker Next Door is the
sweetest baker of them all.
This brown-eyed boy will melt
your heart with his adorable
cupcakes, hundred-watt
smile and incredible charm.
This mouthwatering baker is
definitely the marrying kind.

# Berry Beautiful

This strawberries and cream cupcake will make you feel so berry good that you will be begging for more.

## Strawberries and Cream Cupcakes

MAKES 12

### BERRY CUPCAKES

**Ingredients**

- 1½ cups all-purpose flour
- 1 teaspoon baking powder
- ¼ teaspoon baking soda
- ½ teaspoon salt
- ½ cup (1 stick) unsalted butter, room temperature
- 1 cup sugar
- 1 teaspoon strawberry extract
- ¼ cup strawberry purée (recipe follows)
- ¼ cup heavy cream

1. Preheat oven to 350 degrees F and line 12 muffin cups with paper liners.
2. In a medium bowl, whisk together flour, baking powder, baking soda and salt and set aside.
3. In a large bowl, beat butter and sugar with a mixer until light and fluffy. Add strawberry extract and mix again.
4. Reduce mixer speed to low. Add the dry ingredients to the butter mixture in two parts, alternating with the purée and cream, and mix until all is combined.
5. Evenly fill muffin cups with batter and bake for about 20 minutes or until a toothpick inserted into the center comes out clean. Let cool completely before frosting.

### STRAWBERRY PURÉE

**Ingredients**

- 2 cups fresh strawberries, sliced
- 2 tablespoons sugar

1. Sprinkle strawberries with sugar and set aside until they release their juices, about 30 minutes. Purée in a food processor until smooth.

### STRAWBERRY BUTTERCREAM

**Ingredients**

- ½ cup (1 stick) unsalted butter, room temperature
- 3 cups confectioners' sugar
- 2 tablespoons heavy cream
- 3 tablespoons strawberry purée

1. In a medium bowl, beat the butter with a mixer until smooth. Add sugar, one cup at a time, beating after each addition. Add cream and strawberry purée and mix until smooth.
2. Pipe on top of cooled cupcakes using a pastry bag and tip or plastic bag with the corner snipped off.
3. Cut a strawberry in the shape of a heart and place on top of cupcake.

# Om Nom Nom

This cookie dough cupcake is so serioulsy nummy, it will make you cross-eyed. Be careful, it's as addictive as the Baker Next Door is adorable.

## Cookie Dough Cupcakes with Vanilla Buttercream

MAKES 24

### COOKIE DOUGH CUPCAKES

**Ingredients**

1¾ cups all-purpose flour

1½ teaspoons baking powder

1½ teaspoons baking soda

1 teaspoon salt

1 cup unsweetened cocoa powder

2 cups sugar

2 eggs, room temperature

½ cup vegetable oil

1 cup buttermilk

2 teaspoons vanilla extract

1 cup boiling water

Cookie dough (recipe follows)

1. Preheat oven to 350 degrees F and line 24 muffin cups with paper liners.

2. In a large bowl, whisk together flour, baking powder, baking soda and salt. Stir in cocoa and sugar.

3. In the same bowl, add the eggs, oil, buttermilk and vanilla. Beat with a mixer on a low speed until combined. Add the boiling water and beat for about 1 minute.

4. Fill muffin cups about halfway full with batter, and drop a 1-inch ball of frozen cookie dough into the center of each. Bake for 20-25 minutes or until a toothpick inserted into the center comes out clean. Let cool completely before frosting.

### COOKIE DOUGH

**Ingredients**

1½ cups all-purpose flour

¼ teaspoon baking soda

¼ teaspoon salt

½ cup (1 stick) unsalted butter, melted

½ cup packed brown sugar

¼ cup sugar

¼ cup milk

1 teaspoon vanilla extract

1 cup miniature semisweet chocolate chips

1. In a small bowl, whisk together flour, baking soda and salt and set aside.

2. In a medium bowl, beat the melted butter and sugars with a mixer until combined. Add the milk and vanilla and mix to combine. Add the dry ingredients and mix again. Stir in chocolate chips.

3. Line a baking sheet with parchment paper. Use an ice cream scoop to make 1-inch dough balls. Transfer to the baking sheet and freeze until firm, at least 30 minutes.

### COOKIE MONSTER BUTTERCREAM

**Ingredients**

½ cup (1 stick) unsalted butter, room temperature

3 cups confectioners' sugar

2 tablespoons milk

2 tablespoons blue gel paste

Piping bag with #234 tip

1. In a medium bowl, beat butter with a mixer until light and fluffy. Add sugar, one cup at a time, beating after each addition. Add milk and blend until creamy.

2. Mix blue gel food paste into buttercream until desired color. Fit piping bag with tip and fill with blue frosting.

3. Generously frost the cooled cupcakes with swirls of blue buttercream.

### COOKIE MONSTER DECORATION

Mini chocolate chip cookies

White chocolate candy melts

Black edible marker pen

1. Make a line for the mouth of the cupcake with a butter knife. Break a chocolate chip cookie in half and put it in the mouth.

2. Put eye dots on white chocolate melts with edible marker and place on cupcake.

# Magic Meringue

This lemon meringue cupcake is love in a wrapper.
It's as angelically delicious as our Baker Next Door.

## Lemon Meringue Cupcakes
MAKES 12

### LEMON CUPCAKES

#### Ingredients

2 cups all-purpose flour

1½ teaspoons baking powder

½ teaspoon salt

½ cup (1 stick) unsalted butter, room temperature

1½ cups sugar

2 eggs, room temperature

1 teaspoons vanilla extract

¾ cup buttermilk

1 tablespoon lemon juice

2 tablespoons lemon zest

1. Preheat oven to 350 degrees F and line 12 muffin cups with paper liners.

2. In a medium bowl, whisk together flour, baking powder and salt and set aside.

3. In a large bowl, beat butter and sugar with a mixer until light and fluffy. Add the eggs, one at a time, beating well after each addition. Add vanilla and mix again.

4. Reduce mixer speed to low. Add the dry ingredients to the butter mixture in two parts, alternating with buttermilk, and mix until all is combined. Fold in lemon juice and zest.

5. Evenly fill muffin cups with batter and bake for 18-20 minutes or until a toothpick inserted into the center comes out clean. Let cool completely before frosting or filling.

### LEMON CURD

#### Ingredients

3 eggs, room temperature

¾ cup sugar

⅓ cup fresh lemon juice

4 tablespoons cold unsalted butter

1 tablespoon lemon zest

1. Set a stainless steel bowl over a saucepan of simmering water and whisk together the eggs, sugar and lemon juice until blended. Continue whisking for about 10 minutes until the mixture becomes thick and pale in color. Remove from heat and strain through a fine mesh strainer.

2. Cut the butter into small pieces and whisk, one tablespoon at a time, into the egg mixture until all is combined. Stir in the lemon zest.

3. Cover with plastic wrap, pressing it directly onto the surface of the curd. Refrigerate for at least an hour or up to 24 hours.

4. Spread 1 tablespoon of cooled lemon curd on top of each cupcake. Or, use an apple corer to remove the center of each cupcake and pipe lemon curd into the middle.

### MERINGUE

#### Ingredients

3 egg whites

½ teaspoon cream of tartar

½ cup sugar

1. Preheat oven to 400 degrees F.

2. In a large bowl, beat egg whites and cream of tartar with a mixer on medium speed until soft peaks form. Gradually mix in sugar, one tablespoon at a time. Continue beating until stiff peaks form.

3. Pipe on top of cupcakes using a pastry bag and tip or plastic bag with the corner snipped off. Bake for 5-7 minutes or until meringue is lightly browned. Allow to cool completely before serving. Top with edible butterfly toppers. I bought mine from Incredible Toppers at www.etsy.com.

# Good Guy Vanilla

There are some things that never go out of style, like classic vanilla cupcakes, good guys and a little old-fashioned chivlary.

## Vanilla Cupcakes with Vanilla Buttercream

MAKES 12

### VANILLA CUPCAKES

**Ingredients**

1½ cups all-purpose flour

1½ teaspoons baking powder

½ teaspoon salt

½ cup (1 stick) unsalted butter, room temperature

¾ cup sugar

2 eggs, room temperature

2 teaspoons vanilla extract

½ cup milk

Seeds scraped from one vanilla bean

1. Preheat oven to 350 degrees F and line 12 muffin cups with paper liners.

2. In a medium bowl, whisk together flour, baking powder, and salt and set aside.

1. In a large bowl, beat butter and sugar with a mixer until light and fluffy. Add the eggs, one at a time, beating well after each addition. Add vanilla and mix again.

3. Reduce mixer speed to low. Add the dry ingredients to the butter mixture in two parts, alternating with the milk, and mix until all is combined. Add vanilla seeds and mix again.

4. Evenly fill muffin cups with batter and bake for about 18-20 minutes or until a toothpick inserted into the center comes out clean. Let cool completely before frosting.

### VANILLA BUTTERCREAM

**Ingredients**

½ cup (1 stick) unsalted butter, room temperature

3 cups confectioners' sugar

2 tablespoons milk

1 tablespoon vanilla extract

1 bag M&Ms

1. In a medium bowl, beat butter with a mixer until light and fluffy. Add sugar, one cup at a time, beating after each addition. Add milk and vanilla and blend until creamy.

2. Pipe on top of cooled cupcakes with a pastry bag or plastic bag with the corner snipped off. Decorate with M&Ms.

## Peach Schnapps Cupcakes with Peach Schnapps Frosting

MAKES 12

### PEACH SCHNAPPS CUPCAKES

**Ingredients**

1½ cups all-purpose flour

1½ teaspoons baking powder

½ teaspoon salt

½ cup (1 stick) unsalted butter, room temperature

¾ cup sugar

2 eggs, room temperature

1 teaspoon vanilla extract

¼ cup milk

¼ cup peach schnapps

1. Preheat oven to 350 degrees F and line 12 muffin cups with paper liners.

2. In a medium bowl, whisk together flour, baking powder, and salt and set aside.

3. In a large bowl, beat butter and sugar with a mixer until light and fluffy. Add the eggs, one at a time, beating well after each addition. Add vanilla and mix again.

4. Reduce mixer speed to low. Add the dry ingredients to the butter mixture in two parts, alternating with milk and peach schnapps, and mix until all is combined.

5. Evenly fill muffin cups with batter and bake for about 20 minutes or until a toothpick inserted into the center comes out clean. Let cool completely before frosting.

# I Am Your Superman

This delicious peach flavored cupcake spiked with peach schnapps will make you want to leap tall buildings. It's the best cupcake in Gotham City.

### PEACH SCHNAPPS FROSTING

**Ingredients**

½ cup (1 stick) unsalted butter, room temperature

3 cups confectioners' sugar

3 tablespoons peach schnapps

Blue gel paste food color

1. In a medium bowl, beat the butter with a mixer until creamy. Add sugar, one cup at a time, beating after each addition. Add peach schnapps and beat until light and fluffy. Stir in blue gel paste to desired color.

2. Frost cooled cupcakes using a butter knife to create a smooth surface. Top with an edible Superman cupcake topper.

**To make your own edible Superman toppers, visit the Cupcake Decorations section of my blog at** *ManCandyandCupcakes. com* **for directions.**

# Let's Share a Cone

Smoking hot bakers, ice cream cone cupcakes and Tiffany's boxes tied up with string are a few of my all-time favorite things.

## Ice Cream Cone Cupcakes with Vanila Buttercream Frosting

MAKES 12

### VANILLA CONE CUPCAKES

**Ingredients**

2 eggs, room temperature

1¾ cups cake flour

2 teaspoons baking powder

¼ teaspoon salt

½ cup (1 stick) unsalted butter, room temperature

1 cup sugar, divided

1 teaspoon vanilla extract

½ cup milk

⅛ teaspoon cream of tartar

12 flat-bottom ice cream cones

1. Preheat oven to 350 degrees F.

2. While eggs are cold, separate them, placing the yolks in one bowl and whites in another. Cover the two bowls with plastic wrap and allow the eggs to come to room temperature.

3. In a medium bowl, whisk together cake flour, baking powder and salt and set aside.

4. In a separate bowl, beat butter and ¾ cup of sugar with a mixer until fluffy. Add the egg yolks, one at a time, beating well after each addition. Add vanilla and mix again.

5. Reduce mixer speed to low. Add the dry ingredients to the butter mixture in two parts, alternating with milk, and mix until all is combined.

6. In a clean bowl, beat the egg whites with a mixer until foamy. Add the cream of tarter and beat until soft peaks form. Gradually add the remaining ¼ cup sugar and continue to beat until stiff peaks form. Gently fold the egg whites into the batter until combined. Do not overmix.

7. Fill ice cream cones about two-thirds full with batter. Place cones in a muffin tin and bake for 18-20 minutes or until a toothpick inserted into the center comes out clean. Let cool completely before frosting.

### VANILLA BUTTERCREAM FROSTING

**Ingredients**

½ cup (1 stick) unsalted butter, room temperature

3 cups confectioners' sugar

1 teaspoon vanilla extract

2 tablespoons milk

1. In a medium bowl, beat the butter with a mixer until creamy. Add sugar, one cup at a time, beating after each addition. Add vanilla and milk and mix until light and fluffy.

2. Pipe on top of cooled cupcakes using a pastry bag and tip or plastic bag with the corner snipped off

### CHOCOLATE TOPPING

**Ingredients**

12 ounces semisweet chocolate chips

2 tablespoons canola oil

Multicolored sprinkles

1. In a microwave-safe bowl, combine the chocolate chips and canola oil. Microwave on high for 20-30 seconds at a time, stirring in between, until chocolate is melted. Do not overheat the chocolate.

2. Allow the chocolate to cool slightly. Holding the bottom of a cone, dip the frosted cupcake into the chocolate to coat. Allow the excess chocolate to drip off and add sprinkles. Place in the fridge for 5-10 minutes to harden.

# Everyday Is Sundae

Every day will feel like Sunday when you serve this decadent banana split cupcake. Bake it and watch your date swoon.

## Banana Split Cupcakes with Marshmallow Crème Topping

MAKES 12

### BANANA CUPCAKES

**Ingredients**

- 1½ cups all-purpose flour
- 1 teaspoon baking powder
- ½ teaspoon baking soda
- ¼ teaspoon salt
- ½ cup (1 stick) unsalted butter
- ¾ cup sugar
- 2 eggs, room temperature
- ½ teaspoon vanilla extract
- 1½ cups mashed banana (about 4 ripe bananas)

1. Preheat oven to 350 degrees F and line 12 muffin cups with paper liners.

2. In a medium bowl, whisk together flour, baking powder, baking soda and salt and set aside.

3. In a large bowl, beat butter and sugar with a mixer until light and fluffy. Add the eggs, one at a time, beating well after each addition. Add vanilla and mix again.

4. Reduce mixer speed to low and gradually add the dry ingredients to the butter mixture. Gently fold in the mashed banana. Do not overmix.

5. Evenly fill muffin cups with batter and bake for 20 minutes or until a toothpick inserted into the center comes out clean. Let cool completely before frosting.

### MARSHMALLOW CRÈME TOPPING

**Ingredients**

- 1 cup (2 sticks) unsalted butter, room temperature
- 1 (7-ounce) jar marshmallow crème
- 3 cups confectioners' sugar
- Hot fudge
- 12 maraschino cherries

1. In a medium bowl, beat the butter with a mixer until creamy. Add the marshmallow crème and beat again. Add sugar, one cup at a time, beating after each addition.

2. Pipe on top of cooled cupcakes using a pastry bag with tip or a plastic bag with the corner snipped off. Dribble one tablespoon of hot fudge on top. Garnish with a maraschino cherry.

## Cherry Pie Cupcake with Cherry Cream Cheese Frosting

MAKES 12

### CHERRY PIE CUPCAKES

**Ingredients**

- 1½ cups all-purpose flour
- 1 teaspoon baking powder
- ¼ teaspoon baking soda
- ½ teaspoon salt
- ½ cup buttermilk
- ¼ cup honey
- ½ cup (1 stick) unsalted butter, room temperature
- ¾ cup sugar
- 2 eggs
- 1 teaspoon vanilla extract
- 1 can cherry pie filling

1. Preheat oven to 350 degrees F and line 12 muffin cups with paper liners.

2. In a medium bowl, whisk together flour, baking powder, baking soda and salt and set aside.

3. In a separate bowl, whisk together buttermilk and honey and set aside.

4. In a large bowl, beat butter and sugar with a mixer until light and fluffy. Add the eggs, one at a time, beating well after each addition. Add vanilla and mix again.

5. Reduce mixer speed to low. Add the dry ingredients to the butter mixture in three parts, alternating with the buttermilk-honey mixture, and mix until all is combined.

6. Evenly fill muffin cups with batter and bake for 16-18 minutes or until a toothpick inserted into the center comes out clean. Let cool completely before filling.

7. Once cooled, remove the center of each cupcake with an apple corer, being careful not to pierce the bottom. Spoon about one tablespoon of cherry pie filling into the center of each cupcake.

### CHERRY CREAM CHEESE FROSTING

**Ingredients**

- 8 ounces cream cheese, softened
- ¼ cup (½ stick) unsalted butter, room temperature
- 3 cups confectioners' sugar
- 1 teaspoon vanilla extract
- 2 tablespoons cherry jam
- 1-2 tablespoons milk

1. In a medium bowl, beat cream cheese and butter with a mixer until light and fluffy. Add sugar, one cup at a time, beating after each addition. Add vanilla, cherry jam and milk and mix until incorporated.

2. Pipe on top of cooled cupcakes using a pastry bag and tip or plastic bag with the corner snipped off. Top with a fresh or maraschino cherry.

# You Are My Cherry Pie

Picket fences, cherry pies and the taste of true love are embodied in this mouthwatering cupcake. Bake it if you want to go all the way.

## Blueberry Cupcakes with Blueberry Buttercream

MAKES 12

### BLUEBERRY CUPCAKES

**Ingredients**

1½ cups flour

1 teaspoon baking powder

½ teaspoon baking soda

½ teaspoon salt

½ cup blueberry purée (recipe follows)

½ cup buttermilk

1 teaspoon vanilla extract

½ cup (1 stick) unsalted butter, room temperature

1 cup sugar

2 eggs, room temperature

1 teaspoon lemon zest

.6 ounces freeze-dried blueberries, pulverized in a food processor

1. Preheat oven to 350 degrees F and line 12 muffin cups with paper liners.

2. In a medium bowl, whisk together flour, baking soda, baking powder, and salt and set aside.

3. In another bowl mix together blueberry purée, buttermilk and vanilla extract and set aside.

# Bath-time Blueberry

This scrumptious blueberry cupcake is perfect for enjoying while you scrub-a-dub in the tub. Save water and bathe with a flirtatious friend!

4. In a large bowl, beat butter and sugar with a mixer until light and fluffy. Add the eggs, one at a time, beating well after each addition. Add lemon zest and pulverized dried blueberries and mix until incorporated.

5. Reduce mixer speed to low. Add the dry ingredients to the butter mixture in three parts, alternating with buttermilk mixture, and mix until all is combined.

6. Evenly fill muffin cups with batter and bake for 18-20 minutes or until a toothpick inserted into the center comes out clean. Let cool completely before frosting.

### BLUEBERRY PURÉE

**Ingredients**

1 pint fresh blueberries

1-2 tablespoons water

1. Purée blueberries and water in blender until smooth.

### BLUEBERRY BUTTERCREAM

**Ingredients**

½ cup (1 stick) unsalted butter, room temperature

3 cups confectioners' sugar

¼ cup blueberry purée

1-2 tablespoons milk

1. In a medium bowl, beat the butter with a mixer until creamy. Add sugar, one cup at a time, beating after each addition. Add blueberry purée and milk and mix until light and fluffy.

2. Pipe on top of cooled cupcakes using a pastry bag and tip or plastic bag with the corner snipped off.

**To make your own fondant rubber ducky, visit the Cupcake Decorations section of my blog at *ManCandyandCupcakes. com* for directions.**

# Let's Go Nuts

There's nothing like a bear in the bedroom. This naughty but nice Nutella cupcake is perfect for sharing between the sheets.

## Nutella Cupcakes with Nutella Buttercream

MAKES 12

### NUTELLA CUPCAKES

**Ingredients**

¼ cup unsweetened cocoa powder

½ cup boiling water

½ cup buttermilk

¼ cup heavy cream

1¼ cups all-purpose flour

1 teaspoon baking powder

½ teaspoon baking soda

¼ teaspoon salt

½ cup (1 stick) unsalted butter, room temperature

1 cup sugar

2 eggs, room temperature

1 teaspoon vanilla extract

¼ cup Nutella, room temperature

1. Preheat oven to 350 degrees F and line 12 muffin cups with paper liners.

2. In a small bowl, mix cocoa with boiling water until dissolved. Set aside to cool.

3. In a separate small bowl, whisk together buttermilk and heavy cream and set aside.

4. In a medium bowl, whisk together flour, baking powder, baking soda and salt and set aside.

5. In a large bowl, beat butter and sugar with a mixer until light and fluffy. Add the eggs, one at a time, beating well after each addition. Add vanilla and mix again.

6. Reduce mixer speed to low. Add the flour mixture to the butter mixture in three parts, alternating with the buttermilk mixture, and mix until all is combined.

7. Add the cooled cocoa mixture and beat until smooth. Fold in Nutella.

8. Evenly fill muffins cups with batter and bake for 20-22 minutes or until a toothpick inserted into the center comes out clean. Let cool completely before frosting.

### NUTELLA BUTTERCREAM

**Ingredients**

½ cup (1 stick) unsalted butter, room temperature

3 cups confectioners' sugar

1 teaspoon vanilla extract

1-2 tablespoons milk

¼ cup Nutella

1. In a medium bowl, beat the butter with a mixer until creamy. Add sugar, one cup at a time, beating after each addition. Add vanilla, milk and Nutella and mix until smooth.

2. Pipe on top of cooled cupcakes using a pastry bag and tip or plastic bag with the corner snipped off.

**To make your own fondant teddy bear, visit the Cupcake Decorations section of my blog at** *ManCandyandCupcakes. com* **for directions.**

## Carrot Cupcakes with Orange Cream Cheese Frosting

MAKES 24

### CARROT CUPCAKES

#### Ingredients

2 cups all-purpose flour

1 teaspoon baking soda

1 teaspoon baking powder

¾ teaspoon salt

2 teaspoons ground cinnamon

1½ cup sugar

1 cup olive oil

3 eggs, room temperature

1 teaspoon vanilla extract

½ cup orange juice

3 cups grated carrots

1 cup orange-soaked raisins (recipe follows)

1 cup chopped walnuts

1. Preheat oven to 350 degrees F and line 24 muffin cups with paper liners.

2. In a medium bowl, whisk together flour, baking soda, baking powder, salt and cinnamon and set aside.

3. In a large bowl, beat sugar and oil with a mixer until combined. Add the eggs, one at a time, beating well after each addition. Add vanilla and mix again.

4. Reduce mixer speed to low. Add the dry ingredients to the sugar mixture in two parts, alternating with the orange juice, and mix until all is combined. Fold in grated carrots, raisins and walnuts.

5. Evenly fill muffin cups with batter and bake for 20 minutes or until a toothpick inserted into the center comes out clean. Let cool completely before frosting.

### ORANGE-SOAKED RAISINS

#### Ingredients

1 cup raisins

1 cup orange juice

1. Place raisins in a bowl and pour orange juice over the top. Cover with plastic wrap and refrigerate overnight or for up to 24 hours.

### ORANGE CREAM CHEESE FROSTING

#### Ingredients

8 ounces cream cheese

½ cup (1 stick) unsalted butter, room temperature

3 cups confectioners' sugar

3 tablespoons orange juice

Zest of 1 medium orange

1. In a medium bowl, beat cream cheese and butter with a mixer until creamy.

2. Add sugar, one cup at a time, beating after each addition. Add orange juice and beat again. Fold in orange zest.

3. Allow to chill in the fridge for at least 30 minutes.

4. Pipe on top of cooled cupcakes with a pastry bag and tip or plastic bag with the tip snipped off.

4. Garnish with an edible diamond ring if you like. I ordered mine from Sweet Petal Cottage on Etsy.com.

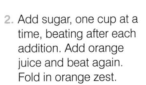

## Six-Carat Cupcake

Nothing says marriage material like a delectable carrot cupcake. It's the cupcake version of the roast dinner. Bake this and watch your lover drop to his knees before you.

# the Castaway Cupcake

The Castaway Cupcake will transport you to deserted beaches and poolside resorts with his holiday-inspired cupcakes. This lusty Latino love hunk will introduce you to a world of forbidden flavors and alfresco fun.

# Coco Loco Cupcake

This tropical cupcake is a vacation in a wrapper.
It's the ideal dessert to enjoy during a beachside tryst.

## Coconut Cupcakes with Coconut Buttercream

MAKES 12

### COCONUT CUPCAKES

**Ingredients**

1½ cups all-purpose flour

1 teaspoon baking powder

½ teaspoon salt

½ cup packed sweetened shredded coconut

½ cup (1 stick) unsalted butter, room temperature

1 cup sugar

3 eggs, room temperature

1 teaspoon coconut extract

¾ cup unsweetened coconut milk

1 teaspoon white vinegar

½ teaspoon baking soda

1. Preheat oven to 350 degrees F and line 12 muffin cups with paper liners.

2. In a medium bowl, whisk together flour, baking powder, salt and shredded coconut and set aside.

3. In a large bowl, beat butter and sugar with a mixer until light and fluffy. Add the eggs, one at a time, beating well after each addition. Add the coconut extract and mix again.

4. Reduce mixer speed to low. Add the dry ingredients to the butter mixture in three parts, alternating with the coconut milk, and mix until all is combined.

5. In a small bowl, combine vinegar and baking soda. (There should be a slight bubbling reaction.) Add to the batter and mix well.

6. Evenly fill muffin cups with batter and bake for 18-20 minutes or until a toothpick inserted into the center comes out clean. Let cool completely before frosting.

### COCONUT BUTTERCREAM

**Ingredients**

½ cup (1 stick) unsalted butter, room temperature

3 cups confectioners' sugar

1½ teaspoons coconut extract

3 tablespoons coconut milk

1. In a medium bowl, beat the butter with a mixer until creamy. Add sugar, one cup at a time, beating after each addition. Add the coconut extract and milk and beat until smooth.

2. Pipe on top of cooled cupcakes using a pastry bag and tip or plastic bag with the corner snipped off.

### COLORED COCONUT

**Ingredients**

14 ounces shredded coconut

Food coloring

Plastic sandwich bags

1. Separate coconut evenly into 4 plastic sandwich bags. Add 6 to 8 drops of your desired food coloring into each bag, seal and shake to mix. You may need to add a few teaspoons of water to help disperse the color evenly.

2. Dip frosted cupcake into the colored coconut to cover.

## Orange Agave Cupcakes with Hibiscus Cream Cheese Frosting

MAKES 12

### ORANGE AGAVE CUPCAKES

**Ingredients**

1½ cups all-purpose flour

1 teaspoon baking powder

¼ teaspoon salt

½ cup (1 stick) unsalted butter, room temperature

¾ cup agave

2 eggs, room temperature

½ teaspoon orange extract

¼ cup coconut cream

¼ cup orange juice

1 tablespoon orange zest

1 teaspoon apple cider vinegar

½ teaspoon baking soda

1. Preheat oven to 350 degrees F and line 12 muffin cups with paper liners.

2. In a medium bowl, whisk together flour, baking powder, and salt and set aside.

3. In a large bowl, beat butter and agave with a mixer until light and fluffy. Add the eggs, one at a time, beating well after each addition. Add orange extract and mix again.

4. Reduce mixer speed to low. Add the dry ingredients to the butter mixture in three parts, alternating with coconut cream and orange juice, and mix until all is combined. Fold in orange zest.

5. In a small bowl, combine vinegar and baking soda. (There should be a slight bubbling reaction.) Add to the batter and mix well.

6. Evenly fill muffin cups with batter and bake for 18-20 minutes or until a toothpick inserted into the center comes out clean. Let cool completely before frosting.

# Petal Power

This orange agave cupcake with fragrant hibiscus cream cheese frosting will take your taste buds on a trip to Nirvana.

### HIBISCUS CREAM CHEESE FROSTING

**Ingredients**

8 ounces cream cheese, softened

½ cup (1 stick) unsalted butter, room temperature

3 cups confectioners' sugar

¼ cup brewed hibiscus tea

1. In a medium bowl, beat cream cheese and butter with a mixer until light and fluffy. Add sugar, one cup at a time, beating after each addition. Slowly add hibiscus tea and beat until incorporated. Chill in the refrigerator.

2. Pipe on top of cooled cupcakes using a pastry bag and tip or plastic bag with the corner snipped off.

3. If you like, top cupcake with a fondant hibiscus flower made from a silicon candy mold. Roll white fondant to create the flower details.

# Sexy Hot Chocolate

These chili chocolate cupcakes will put you in the mood for some red hot loving. You will be panting for more.

## Chili Chocolate Cupcakes with Chili Chocolate Buttercream

MAKES 12

### CHILI CHOCOLATE CUPCAKES

**Ingredients**

½ cup (1 stick) unsalted butter, room temperature

2 ounces semisweet chocolate chips

½ cup unsweetened cocoa powder

1 cup all-purpose flour

1 teaspoon baking powder

½ teaspoon baking soda

½ teaspoon salt

1 teaspoon chili powder

1 teaspoon cayenne

1 teaspoon cinnamon

2 eggs, room temperature

½ cup sugar

¼ cup packed light brown sugar

1 teaspoon vanilla extract

½ cup sour cream

1. Preheat oven to 350 degrees F and line 12 muffin cups with paper liners.

2. Put the butter and chocolate chips in a microwave-safe bowl and microwave on high, 30 seconds at a time, until melted. Stir until smooth and set aside to cool slightly.

3. In a medium bowl, whisk together cocoa, flour, baking powder, baking soda, salt, chili powder, cayenne and cinnamon and set aside.

4. In a large bowl, beat eggs, sugars and vanilla with a mixer until combined. Add cooled chocolate mixture and beat until smooth.

5. Reduce mixer speed to low. Add the dry ingredients to the chocolate mixture in three parts, alternating with the sour cream, and mix until just combined. Do not overmix.

6. Evenly fill muffin cups with batter and bake for 16-18 minutes or until a toothpick inserted into the center comes out clean. Let cool completely before frosting.

### CHILI CHOCOLATE BUTTERCREAM

**Ingredients**

½ cup unsweetened cocoa powder

½ cup (1 stick) unsalted butter, room temperature

3½ cups confectioners' sugar

2 teaspoons chili powder

2 tablespoons milk

Cayenne pepper, for garnish

1. In a medium bowl, beat cocoa and butter until creamy. Add sugar, one cup at a time, beating after each addition. Add chili powder and milk and beat until smooth.

2. Pipe onto cupcakes using a pastry bag and tip or plastic bag with the corner snipped off. Garnish with cayenne pepper.

### FONDANT RED CHILI

**Ingredients**

Red fondant

Green fondant

1 inch daisy fondant cutter mold

Small paint brush

1. Form the red fondant into a chili shape. Roll out green fondant to ⅛ inch thickness and cut out a daisy shape using the daisy fondant flower cutter to form the top of the chili.

2. Dip the paintbrush in water and brush the bottom of the green top to make it sticky. Attach it to the red chili.

3. Roll a small ball of green fondant into a tiny stem and attach to the chili top. Put fondant chili in the fridge to firm before placing on cupcake.

# A Good Catch

This sweet potato cupcake with spicy cream cheese frosting will make you feel as if you were carousing in the Caribbean.

## Jamaican Sweet Potato Cupcakes with Spiced Cream Cheese Frosting
MAKES 24

### JAMAICAN SWEET POTATO CUPCAKES

**Ingredients**

2 cups all-purpose flour

1 teaspoon baking powder

1 teaspoon baking soda

¾ teaspoon salt

1 teaspoon cinnamon

½ teaspoon ginger

½ teaspoon nutmeg

½ teaspoon allspice

1½ cup brown sugar

1 cup coconut oil

3 eggs, room temperature

1 teaspoon vanilla extract

½ cup coconut cream

2 tablespoons rum

3 cups grated sweet potato

1 cup rum-soaked raisins (recipe follows)

1. Preheat oven to 350 degrees F and line 24 muffin cups with paper liners.

2. In a medium bowl, whisk together flour, baking powder, baking soda, salt, cinnamon, ginger, nutmeg and allspice and set aside.

3. In a large bowl, beat sugar and coconut oil with a mixer until combined. Add the eggs, one at a time, beating well after each addition. Add vanilla and mix again.

4. Reduce mixer speed to low. Add the dry ingredients to the sugar mixture in two parts, alternating with coconut cream and rum, and mix until all is combined. Fold in grated sweet potato and raisins.

5. Evenly fill muffin cups with batter and bake for 20 minutes or until a toothpick inserted into the center comes out clean. Let cool completely before frosting.

### RUM-SOAKED RAISINS

**Ingredients**

1 cup raisins

¼ cup rum

1. Place raisins in a bowl and pour rum over the top. Cover with plastic wrap and place in the fridge for at least 2 hours and up to 24 hours before using.

### SPICED CREAM CHEESE FROSTING

**Ingredients**

8 ounces cream cheese, softened

½ cup (1 stick) unsalted butter, room temperature

3 cups confectioners' sugar

½ teaspoon cinnamon

¼ teaspoon ginger

¼ teaspoon nutmeg

¼ teaspoon allspice

1. In a medium bowl, beat cream cheese and butter with a mixer until light and fluffy. Add sugar, one cup at a time, beating after each addition. Add spices and mix to combine.

2. Pipe on top of cooled cupcakes using a pastry bag and tip or plastic bag with the corner snipped off.

**To make your own edible clownfish, visit the Cupcake Decorations section of my blog at** *ManCandyandCupcakes. com* **for directions.**

This moist mango cupcake will make you starry-eyed for your significant other and put you in the mood to ride the waves of passion.

## Mango Tapioca-Filled Mango Cupcakes with Mango Frosting

MAKES 12

### MANGO CUPCAKES

**Ingredients**

1½ cups all-purpose flour

1 teaspoon baking powder

½ teaspoon salt

½ cup (1 stick) butter, room temperature

1 cup sugar

2 eggs, room temperature

1 teaspoon vanilla extract

½ cup mango purée (recipe follows)

1 teaspoon white vinegar

½ teaspoon baking soda

1. Preheat oven to 350 degrees F and line 12 muffin cups with paper liners.

2. In a medium bowl, whisk together flour, baking powder, and salt and set aside.

3. In a large bowl, beat butter and sugar with a mixer until light and fluffy. Add the eggs, one a time, beating well after each addition. Add vanilla and mix again.

4. Reduce mixer speed to low. Add the dry ingredients to the butter mixture in two parts, alternating with the mango purée, and mix until all is combined.

5. In a small bowl, combine vinegar and baking soda. (There should be a slight bubbling reaction.) Add to the batter and mix well.

6. Evenly fill muffin cups with batter and bake for 18-20 minutes or until a toothpick inserted into the center comes out clean. Let cool completely before filling and frosting.

### MANGO PURÉE

**Ingredients**

3 ripe mangoes, peeled, pitted and cut into chunks

½ cup sugar

3 tablespoons water

1. Combine all ingredients in a blender and purée until smooth. Use ½ cup in cupcakes and reserve the rest for filling and frosting.

### MANGO TAPIOCA FILLING

**Ingredients**

⅓ cup sugar

3 tablespoons instant tapioca

¾ cup milk

2 cups reserved mango purée

1 egg, beaten

1. In a medium saucepan, combine sugar, tapioca, milk, mango purée and egg and let stand for five minutes.

2. Bring the mixture to a boil over medium heat, stirring constantly. Remove from heat and allow to cool completely before using.

### MANGO FROSTING

**Ingredients**

½ cup (1 stick) unsalted butter, room temperature

3 cups confectioners' sugar

3 tablespoons mango purée

1. In a medium bowl, beat the butter with a mixer until smooth. Add sugar, one cup at a time, beating after each addition. Add the mango purée and beat until light and fluffy.

### ASSEMBLY

1. When cupcakes are cool, use an apple corer to remove the center of each cupcake, being careful not to pierce the bottom.

2. Scoop about 1 tablespoon of cooled tapioca mixture into each cupcake. Pipe mango frosting on top using a pastry bag and tip or plastic bag with the corner snipped off.

**To make your own edible starfish, visit the Cupcake Decorations section of my blog at** *ManCandyandCupcakes. com* **for directions.**

## Pina Colada Cupcakes with Coconut Rum Buttercream

MAKES 12

### PINA COLADA CUPCAKES

**Ingredients**

2 cups all-purpose flour

1 teaspoon baking powder

½ teaspoon salt

½ cup (1 stick) unsalted butter, room temperature

1½ cups sugar

3 eggs, room temperature

1 teaspoon vanilla extract

1½ cups canned pineapple pieces, crushed

1 teaspoon white vinegar

½ teaspoon baking soda

1. Preheat oven to 350 degrees F and line 12 muffin cups with paper liners.

2. In a medium bowl, whisk together the flour, baking powder and salt and set aside.

3. In a large bowl, beat butter and sugar with a mixer until light and fluffy. Add the eggs, one at a time, beating well after each addition. Add vanilla and mix again.

4. Reduce mixer speed to low. Add the dry ingredients to the butter mixture in two parts, alternating with crushed pineapple, and mix until all is combined.

5. In a small bowl, combine vinegar and baking soda. (There should be a slight bubbling reaction.) Add to the batter and mix well.

6. Evenly fill muffin cups with batter and bake for 18-20 minutes or until a toothpick inserted into the center comes out clean. Let cool completely before frosting.

### COCONUT RUM BUTTERCREAM

**Ingredients**

½ cup (1 stick) unsalted butter, room temperature

3 cups confectioners' sugar

1 teaspoon coconut extract

2 tablespoons light rum

½ cup sweetened shredded coconut, for topping

1. In a medium bowl, beat the butter with a mixer until smooth. Add sugar, one cup at a time, beating after each addition. Add coconut extract and rum and beat until combined.

2. Pipe on top of cooled cupcakes using a pastry bag and tip or plastic bag with the corner snipped off. Top with shredded coconut. If you like, top with a fondant pineapple made from a silicon candy mold.

# PiNa CoLada Party TiMe

This Pina Colada cupcake is the perfect way to start a party for two. It will make you want to do the horizontal conga.

This delicious caramelized plantain cupcake will tantalize your taste buds and unleash a tidal wave of lust.

## Caramelized Plantain Cupcakes with Rum Buttercream

MAKES 12

### CARAMELIZED PLANTAIN CUPCAKES

**Ingredients**

2 cups all-purpose flour

1 teaspoon baking powder

1 teaspoon baking soda

½ teaspoon salt

½ cup (1 stick) unsalted butter, room temperature

1½ cups sugar

2 eggs, room temperature

1 teaspoon vanilla extract

1 cup buttermilk

2 cups mashed caramelized plantains (recipe follows)

1. Preheat oven to 350 degrees F and line 12 muffin cups with paper liners.

2. In a medium bowl, whisk together flour, baking powder, baking soda and salt and set aside.

3. In a large bowl, beat butter and sugar with a mixer until light and fluffy. Add the eggs, one at a time, beating well after each addition. Add vanilla and mix again.

4. Reduce mixer speed to low. Add the dry ingredients to the butter mixture in two parts, alternating with the buttermilk, and mix until all is combined. Fold in mashed plantains.

5. Evenly fill muffin cups with batter and bake for 18-20 minutes or until a toothpick inserted into the center comes out clean. Let cool completely before frosting.

### CARAMELIZED PLANTAINS

**Ingredients**

2 tablespoons butter, melted

3 tablespoons brown sugar

½ teaspoon cinnamon

3 very ripe plantains (peels should be brown or black), peeled and sliced into ½-inch pieces

1. Preheat oven to 400 degrees F.

2. In a small bowl, combine melted butter, brown sugar and cinnamon. Place plantains in a small baking dish and pour the mixture over the top.

3. Bake for about 20 minutes, until plantains are soft and caramelized. Remove from oven and mash with a fork, reserving 12 whole pieces for garnish.

### RUM BUTTERCREAM

**Ingredients**

½ cup (1 stick) unsalted butter, room temperature

3 cups confectioners' sugar

3 tablespoons light rum

1. In a medium bowl, beat the butter with a mixer until smooth. Add sugar, one cup at a time, beating after each addition. Add rum and mix to combine.

2. Pipe on top of cooled cupcakes using a pastry bag and tip or plastic bag with the corner snipped off. Top with a slice of caramelized plantain.

**To make your own edible surfboard, visit the Cupcake Decorations section of my blog at** *Mancandyandcupcakes. com* **for directions.**

# Margarita Mayhem

This margarita cupcake will put you in the mood to make mad, passionate love long into the night.

## Margarita Cupcakes with Lime Cream Cheese Frosting

MAKES 12

### MARGARITA CUPCAKES

**Ingredients**

2 ounces tequila

1 ounce triple sec

1 ounce lime juice

1 ½ cups all-purpose flour

1 ½ teaspoons baking powder

½ teaspoon salt

½ cup (1 stick) unsalted butter, room temperature

1 cup sugar

2 eggs, room temperature

1 teaspoon orange extract

2 teaspoons lime zest

¼ cup buttermilk

1. Preheat oven to 350 degrees F and line 12 muffin cups with paper liners.

2. Combine tequila, triple sec and lime juice to make a margarita cocktail and set aside.

3. In a medium bowl, whisk together flour, baking powder and salt and set aside.

4. In a large bowl, beat butter and sugar with a mixer until light and fluffy. Add the eggs, one at a time, beating well after each addition. Add orange extract and lime zest and mix to combine.

5. Reduce mixer speed to low. Add the dry ingredients to the butter mixture in three parts, alternating with the margarita and buttermilk, and mix until all is combined.

6. Evenly fill muffin cups with batter and bake for 18-20 minutes or until a toothpick inserted into the center comes out clean. Let cool completely before frosting.

### LIME CREAM CHEESE FROSTING

**Ingredients**

8 ounces cream cheese

½ cup (1 stick) unsalted butter, room temperature

3-4 tablespoons Rose's lime juice

4-5 cups confectioners' sugar

Lime slices, for garnish

Paper umbrellas, for garnish

1. In a medium bowl, beat cream cheese and butter with a mixer until light and fluffy. Add sugar, one cup at a time, beating after each addition. Add the Rose's lime juice and mix to combine.

2. Pipe on top of cooled cupcakes using a pastry bag and tip or plastic bag with the corner snipped off. Garnish with a lime slice and little umbrella.

## Tia Maria Cupcakes with Tia Maria Buttercream

MAKES 12

### TIA MARIA CUPCAKES

**Ingredients**

- 1½ cups all-purpose flour
- 1½ teaspoons baking powder
- ½ teaspoon salt
- ½ cup (1 stick) unsalted butter, room temperature
- ¾ cup sugar
- 2 large eggs, room temperature
- 1 teaspoon vanilla extract
- ¼ cup sweetened condensed milk
- ¼ cup Tia Maria

1. Preheat oven to 350 degrees F and line 12 muffin cups with paper liners.

2. In a medium bowl, whisk together flour, baking powder, and salt and set aside.

3. In a large bowl, beat butter and sugar with a mixer until light and fluffy. Add the eggs, one at a time, beating well after each addition. Add vanilla and mix again.

4. Reduce mixer speed to low. Add the dry ingredients to the butter mixture in two parts, alternating with condensed milk and Tia Maria, and mix until all is combined.

5. Evenly fill muffin cups with batter and bake for 18-20 minutes or until a toothpick inserted into the center comes out clean. Let cool completely before frosting.

### TIA MARIA WHIPPED BUTTERCREAM

**Ingredients**

- ½ cup (1 stick) unsalted butter
- 3 cups confectioners' sugar
- 2 tablespoons Tia Maria

1. In a medium bowl, beat the butter with a mixer until smooth. Add sugar, one cup at a time, beating after each addition. Add the Tia Maria and mix to combine.

2. Frost cooled cupcakes using a butter knife to create a smooth surface. Top with edible topper.

**To make your own edible tropical sunset topper, visit the Cupcake Decorations section of my blog at** *Mancandyandcupcakes.com* **for directions.**

## Sunset Dreams

This Tia Maria cupcake will make you want to walk off hand in hand into the sunset with your lover and lose yourself in his soft caress.

# THE cupcake COWBOY

# the Bad Boy BAKER

Apple Cider Cupcakes with Apple
Cider Cream Cheese Frosting - **18**

Banana Walnut Cupcakes with
Chocolate Molasses Frosting - **28**

Blue Velvet Cupcakes with Jack
Daniel's Cream Cheese Frosting - **20**

Bread Pudding Cupcakes with
Cinnamon Cream Cheese Frosting - **25**

Chocolate Bourbon Cupcakes with
Whiskey Chocolate Buttercream - **12**

Hazelnut Cupcakes with Espresso
Frangelico Buttercream - **15**

Jalapeño Peach Cupcakes with
Peach Cream Cheese Frosting - **23**

Maple Cheesecake Cupcakes
with Strawberry Sauce - **26**

Reese's Peanut Butter Cupcakes
with Peanut Butter Frosting - **11**

Salted Caramel Cupcakes with
Caramel Buttercream - **08**

Spiced Pumpkin Cupcakes
with Cream Cheese Frosting - **16**

Beer Cupcakes with
Caramel Frosting - **35**

Coffee and Donut Cupcakes
with Coffee Frosting - **47**

Dark and Stormy Cupcakes with
Lime Cream Cheese Frosting - **39**

Devil's Food Cupcakes
with Midnight Ganache - **48**

Licorice Cupcakes with Vanilla
Sambuca Buttercream - **40**

Mudslide Cupcakes with Kahlua
and Bailey's Buttercream Swirl - **45**

Pound Cupcakes with
Amaretto Buttercream - **32**

Raspberry Jello Shot Cupcakes with
Raspberry Vanilla Buttercream - **42**

Red Velvet Cupcakes with
Cognac Cream Cheese Frosting - **36**

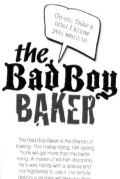

The fastest froster in the Wild West!

# THE cupcake COWBOY

This bronco-busting baker is at home behind the range. His homespun cupcakes will have you chomping at the bit for more

Go on. Take a bite! I know you want to

# the Bad Boy BAKER

The Bad Boy Baker is the Brando of baking. This Harley-riding, hell-raising hunk will get more than the batter rising. A master of kitchen discipline, he's very handy with a spatula and not frightened to use it. His sinfully delicious recipes will take you from bike to bar room to the bedroom. Being bad never tasted so good!

30 MAN CANDY & CUPCAKES

# the boy next door

# the CastaWay cupcake

Can I borrow some sugar, sugar?

## the boy next door

The Baker Next Door is the
sweetest baker of them all.
This brown-eyed boy will melt
your heart with his adorable
cupcakes, hundred-watt
smile and incredible charm.
This mouthwatering baker is
definitely the marrying kind.

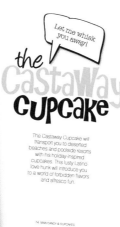

Let me whisk you away!

## the CastaWay cupcake

The Castaway Cupcake will
transport you to deserted
beaches and poolside resorts
with his holiday-inspired
cupcakes. This lusty Latino
love hunk will introduce you
to a world of forbidden flavors
and alfresco fun.

74. MAN CANDY & CUPCAKES

# WITH FONDANT MEMORIES

It takes a lot more than a vivid imagination and a dirty mind to create a cupcake book packed tighter than Marky Mark's Calvins with sexy shirtless men and seductive recipes. And I couldn't have created this abtastic opus all on my own.

There are several people who were instrumental in bringing this bodacious book to life. The first of which is my fabulous editor **Christa Bourg**, the wind beneath my literary wings. She helped me develop the book from a mad idea into a mouthwatering tome and was an endless source of sage advice.

I also roped in my friend and neighbor, the adorable **Rebecca Ellman**, to help with all the logistics of putting this titillating tome together, from casting my buffed bakers, to testing recipes, to assisting with photography. No matter the task I gave her, from applying baby oil to mixing batter, Rebecca did it with alacrity. When she is not being conscripted into one of my crazy ideas, she runs her own catering business, Rebecca Elman Catering.

The delightful and dashing **Noah Weintraub** assisted on the location shoots, lending his skills and sunny disposition to ensure they went smoothly. I also owe a big thanks to the lovely **Jean Weil** who loaned us the use of her pool for the Castaway pics and was wonderfully hospitable. Thanks also to **Iris Weintraub** who let us stash our supplies at her beach house.

I owe a big shout-out to my designer **Sharon Metzl** who did an amazing job putting the book together. Shazza helped me make *Man Candy and Cupcakes* the sexiest book to hit the shelves since the Kama Sutra. **Trina Johnson** also did a fantastic job redesigning my website. A big hug also goes to my friend and legal eagle **Neil Weinrib** (aka "The Oracle").

Of course, I have to give a big kiss and a squeeze to the fabulous baker boys: **Brad Belk**, **Geronimo Frias**, **Davide Filippini** and **Thomas Whitfield**. They are not only drool-worthy but a delight to work with. Even thinking about them makes me want to take a cold shower.

Finally, thank you to all my Kickstarter pledgers whose generosity and encouragement helped me bring this abtastic book to fruition.

Bon Appétit!

*Babe* ♡

# ABOUT THE AUTHOR

Kitchen vixen, *Babe Scott*, is on a mission to put the flirt into food and the brawn into baking. Her latest book Man Candy and Cupcakes was a labor of lust, but this culinary auteur tackled it with the same zeal Cher has when she conquers the stage at Caesar's Palace. *Babe* tracked down the world's sexiest men, invented her own provocative flavor profiles, styled and photographed the bakers, and even administered the suntan lotion where required.

This stovetop siren is also the author of an entertaining guide for the domestically challenged titled **The Lazy Hostess**. This titillating tome was published in the UK and Australia by Transworld and will be launched in the U.S. in 2015 by *Babe*'s own imprint, **Babe Media**. The **Lazy Hostess** puts the curve into cocktail parties by showing readers how to host a sizzling soiree without stretching the wallet or inducing a stress headache. Most importantly, it ensures that the hostess looks and feels like a supernova.

*Babe* is also a card-carrying manthropologist, having previously authored **Delicious Dating**, a book that reveals what you can tell about a man's bedroom style from his dining style. *Babe* has aired her saucy views on dating and mating across the U.S. with appearances on **Good Day New York**, **Pix11 News**, **7 Live San Francisco**, **Fox 25 Boston**, **WGN Chicago**, and a plethora of other shows.

Her dating adventures and insights have also been recounted in **The New York Daily News**, **Glamour**, **The Guardian**, **Good Housekeeping**, **BBC World News**, **Match.com**, **Cupid's Pulse**, **MSN Lifestyle**, **Perez Hilton.com**, **Fushion magazine**, **CNN Living**, **Instinct Magazine**, and many other popular sites. *Babe* is also a sought-after radio guest with her compelling combination of sassy advice and tongue-in-chic humor and has appeared on numerous programs both in the U.S. and abroad.

This kitchen vixen blogs for **The Huffington Post** and has written for a smorgasbord of online publications, including **Glamour**, **CNN Living**, **Yahoo!Shine**, **Buzzfeed**, **Elle Australia**, **Your Tango**, **She Said**, and many other popular sites.

For more servings of *Babe*'s hunky men, risqué recipes and tongue-in-chic humor, visit her website at **BabeScott.com**.